The baneful existence of Chinese sea cucumber farms
In Sri Lanka

By
Asanga Abeyagoonasekera

Published By South Asia Foresight Network (SAFN)

The Millennium Project Washington DC

South Asia Foresight Network Monographic Series
Volume 1
4421 Garrison Street, N.W. Washington, D.C. 20016-4055

First published in Washington DC 2023 March
This edition published 2023 March

"What we have now - a world without marine reserves - is like a debit account where we withdraw all the time, and we never make any deposit. Reserves are like savings accounts."

Enric Sala, National Geographic Explorer

Table of Contents

Introduction

My interest in the beautiful sea surrounding Sri Lanka was from childhood. After the Asian Tsunami in 2004 I was engaged in the reconstruction of the coastal belt, the fishery harbours of Sri Lanka. With enormous assistance from US, Japan, China, and many other nations and non-governmental organizations the coastal infrastructure was restored in less than three years. As the Chairman of the countries fishery harbours corporation (CFHC)[1], I learned the value of our Ocean resources from many local fisherman and academics at NARA[2]. The marine eco system to the island is an important link, such as an umbilical cord that connects mother to a child. When the ecosystem is threatened by human action the consequences are long-term impacting generations. The marine resource plunder such as sea cucumber overexploitation taking place in Sri Lanka is a direct threat to the marine ecosystem. According to Dr. Bondaroff a world expert in illegal fishing, 'As deposit feeders, sea cucumbers play an important role in nutrient cycling. Their actions reduce organic loads and redistribute surface sediment, and the inorganic nitrogen and phosphorus they excrete enhances the benthic habitat. In this way, they make excellent bioremediators. These same actions increase seawater alkalinity, which helps create local buffers against ocean acidification, supporting the survival of coral reefs'[3].

Sri Lankan coral reefs in the South had the worse impact from hundreds of motorized boats, destroying the reefs. Today the sea cucumber an important marine animal contributing to achieve a balance in the ocean life is threatened in Sri Lanka. This report will assess the present threat to sea cucumber in Sri Lanka and destruction of the marine environment by human interaction with support extended by China.

Geopolitics and Marine Resource

The ocean sphere is an integral factor in geopolitics. The surrounding marine resources of an Island are part of its geography. The island nation of Sri Lanka geostrategically located in the Indian ocean, possesses a territorial sea of 21,500 sq.km and an Exclusive Economic Zone (EEZ) of up to 200 nautical miles (370 km) from the coastal line an extent of 517,000 sq.km. Sri Lanka has the rights to the resources in the water column, seabed and subsurface in the EEZ. Under the UN Law of the Sea, Sri Lanka is entitled to claim for an extended area of seabed where the thickness of the sediment layer exceeds 1 km. The UN claim was developed and submitted by Sri Lankan government during my tenure at the fishery harbours corporation[4]. If accepted, the EEZ will expand further with the delimitation of the outer edge of the continental margin of the country, which would permit Sri Lanka to own an EEZ equivalent to 23 times (approximately 1.400,000 km2) the size of its land mass. The extended wide area of ocean contains a variety of exploitable minerals and hydrocarbons[5] where geopolitical interest and competition could rise over time by extra-regional powers in Sri Lanka's marine sphere. Since China dominates supply chains for all critical minerals including nickel, cobalt, lithium, copper, and the rare earths, the interest in extracting polymetallic nodules from the deep seabed is the next possible resource venture.

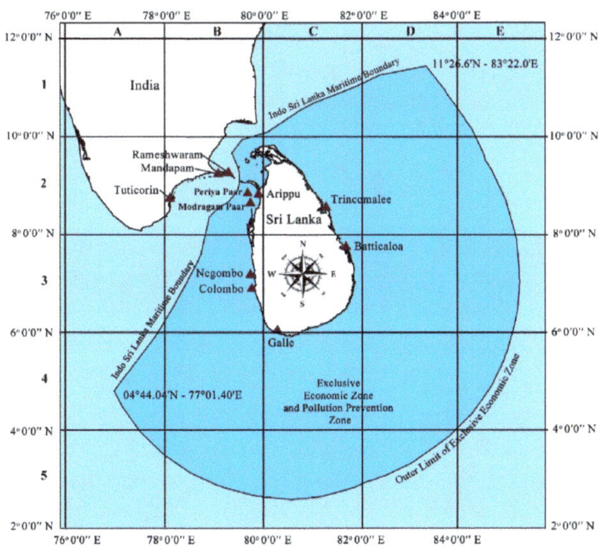

Map of the Sri Lankan Exclusive Economic Zone (EEZ) (Source: Maritime Boundaries Geodatabase, Flanders Marine Institute)[6].

In the present Sri Lanka is facing its worst Economic crisis since its independence in 1948. Sri Lanka faces a significant Chinese influence in the recent past, from its infrastructure projects in the south and western quarters of the island. China is one of the largest creditors with 3.5 billion of outstanding loans. Some Chinese projects seen as economically beneficial failed to generate the expected revenue and jobs. These projects have become a burden to the ailing economy. Chinese land acquisitions from long-term lease agreements for 99 years in Hambanthota port and Colombo Port City raised many concerns, where none of these lease agreements was made available to the public. On Hambanthota port lease, according to former Minister Mahinda Samarasinghe who presently serves as the Sri Lankan ambassador in Washington DC said "we managed to reduce the duration of 99 years, but we were never given an option from Beijing for an alternative to settle our debt, President Xi said lease the port, and that is it"[7]. While environmental impact assessments (EIA) for most Chinese projects have raised concerns such as Port City and Mattala airport[8] built near a wildlife sanctuary, Chinese companies have managed to bypass the regulatory framework by building political agency with local politicians.

With the rising food and kerosine prices which quadrupled to 340 rupees, unbearable to the public and to the fisheries industry, a lucrative business from Chinese 'sea cucumber firm' has offered a solution to farm sea cucumber and earn a better pay to the local fisher community[9]. While the Indian trawlers and boats with illegal practices in the northern waters is a concern, the sea cucumber farming is not the alternative solution for the island nation.

Chinese interest in the marine resources is already a concern in the pacific. According to Beijing's *distant-water fishing fleet* report, ships fishing outside of internationally recognized exclusive economic zones (EEZs), numbered 2,701 ships in 2020, easily making it the world's largest[10] argues Derek Grossman at RAND[11]. Further adding 'The problem is that in order to satisfy the tastes of China's burgeoning middle class, Beijing——without respect for international commercial and environmental standards—incentivizes fleets to haul in as much seafood as possible (tuna and sea cucumbers, in particular), resulting in massive numbers of illegal, unreported, and unregulated (IUU) fishing incidents'. Palau discovered and deported 28 Chinese fishermen poaching sea creatures within its EEZ[12].

The same is visible in the South Pacific around American Samoa[13] and as far east as the Galapagos Islands[14]. In the waters of Sri Lanka and India there has been multiple arrests relating to the sea cucumber trade.

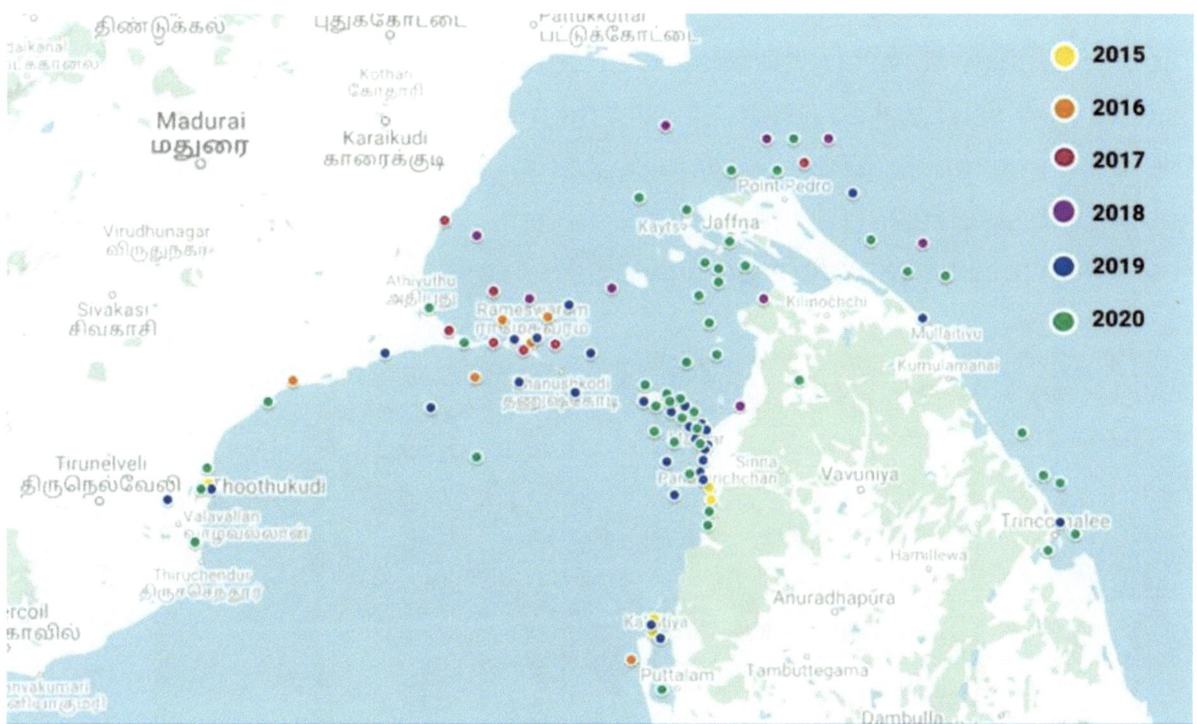

This map shows the locations where arrests and seizures relating to the sea cucumber trade were carried out from 2015-2020. Image courtesy of OceansAsia[15].

The Chinese Ambassador Qi Zhenhong visited the northern fisheries community[16] distributing rations and promising hope and a better income to the community. While Chinese maneuvers in India's immediate periphery will be a concern to New Delhi's security, Chinese sea cucumber venture approved by Sri Lankan government will create another geopolitical concern to India and Sri Lanka. For Sri Lanka, it's important to consider long term marine ecological and environment harm from IUU fishing and sea cucumber farming and request international assistance to preserve its delicate marine environment for the future generations.

Marine Resource

Sea urchins

Sea urchin (scientific name: *Echinoidea*) are aquatic marine animals with round, globular spiny bodies. Unable to swim, these spiky creatures are found at the seabed. Their hard outer skeleton which is called a test, protect them from predators such as eels and otters. Like the other members of the echinoidea family, sea urchins also display five-point symmetry in its skeleton. The test of sea urchins is covered with spines, also called radioles, which may be very different in form from one group to another.

Sea urchins are omnivores that feed on anything that floats in their vicinity. This may include plankton, kelp, periwinkles and in rare cases, even barnacles and mussels.[17] They use their sharp teeth to scrape algae off the underwater rocks.

Sea urchins are commercially valuable marine animals that are consumed mostly in China, Hong Kong, Taiwan, and Singapore. These animals are cultivated around the globe in temperate waters of North America, North Pacific, Chile, and New Zealand and recently in Sri Lanka.[18] The high value of sea urchins is justified by their low supply; they are harvested only during the non-spawning season. This makes them a prized delicacy for gonad lovers who can pay the top dollar to enjoy the creamiest high-quality sea urchin.

Sea cucumber

Unlike its namesake, sea cucumbers are not plants but marine animals. Sea cucumbers (*Holothuroidea*) are a relative of Sea urchins and star fishes and belong to the same family of *echinoderms*. Unlike sea urchins, sea cucumbers have a long, barrel shaped body with soft, leathery skin.

Being scavengers, sea cucumber mainly feed on zooplanktons and tiny particles of algae found on the seabed. Sometimes, they burrow and ingest detritus buried in the sediment using tube feet that surround their mouths.

Sea cucumbers are only found in salt water and have more than a thousand species around the world. However, only about two dozen of them are considered commercially valuable. Considered a delicacy in Southeast Asia, these nutritious animals are also consumed as medicines to treat muscle fatigue, impotence, joint pain and enhancing sports performance among others. They are rich in protein, calcium, potassium, zinc, iron, selenium, manganese, amino acids, and antioxidants but don't have any cholesterol.

They play a vital role in conserving and sustaining the marine ecology and for that they are also termed as 'earthworms of the sea'. Sea cucumbers help detoxify contaminants in the soil and other environments, help in nutrient cycling and redistribution of sediments. Moreover, they help other species such as corals to live, which makes sea cucumbers ideal for bioremediation.

Favorable weather in Sri Lanka

Sea cucumber farming was introduced in Sri Lanka by the Chinese many centuries ago. In 1917, the English zoologist James Hornell noted that the sea cucumber trade between India, Sri Lanka, and China is at least 1,000 years old. It was one of the main commodities that were commercially sold to China through the ancient silk route. While Sea cucumbers have been a staple in China for centuries, proper aquaculture was developed only in the 20th century by Zhang Fenying. By 1980s, thanks to the socioeconomic boom and increased awareness about the nutritional content of the animal, the market demand for it grew exponentially.

In recent times, due to the rise in demand in China and Chinese communities present world-wide, Sri Lanka is emerging as the hub for sea cucumber farming. The largest fish breeding sites are located near shallow coastal lands due to favorable marine environment including sunlight and sea plants.

Picture from NAQDA [19]

Sea cucumbers being dried in preparation for export. Photo courtesy of Ganeshan Nishanthan[20].

Traditional ways of fishing sea cucumbers and sea urchins

When the Chinese introduced sea cucumber harvesting in Sri Lanka approximately a millennium ago, sea cucumbers were harvested by hand during the low tide periods walking along the shallow coastal areas of northern and north-western coasts of Sri Lanka. Gradually over the period, a few techniques were developed by the locals to make the harvesting process a little more efficient.

One of those traditional techniques is harvesting sea cucumbers using wooden *vallam* and *siraku valai*, a passive type of fishing gear which is set up in night and harvested the following morning. This method has been popular in shallow waters and near shore areas. Another traditional method is *patti valai*, which is used to harvest fish and prawn using square-shaped nets.[21]

In addition, sea cucumbers were easily picked up by divers, who dive from traditional *oru*, a type of canoe, small boats, catamarans, and pedal boats. Divers used to engage in breath-hold freediving using no or minimal equipment that includes a glass mask, an aluminum plate flipper, and a bag to collect the catch. However, this labor-intensive activity that demands the diver to be gentle and skillful was limited to near shore areas and shallow waters.

Another method of sea cucumber harvesting is gleaning which is mostly practiced by women and children walking from shore to the shallow waters. Gleaning is a fishing method used in shallow coastal areas and habitats that are exposed during low tide.

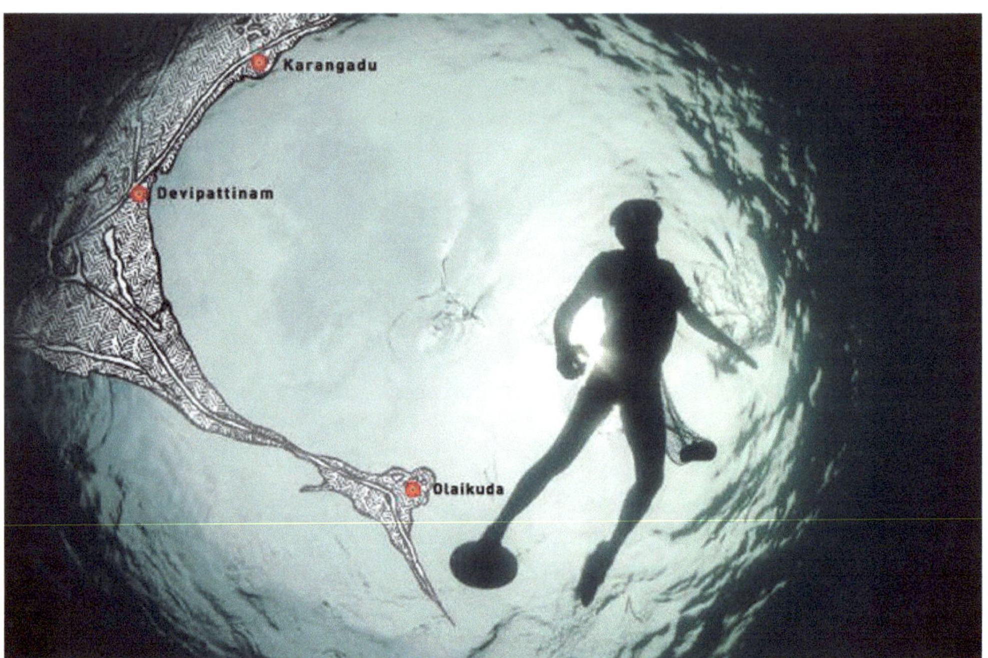

Photo courtesy of Umeed Mistry[22]

Sea cucumbers were common in shallow coastal waters decades ago, but divers say they now have to go deeper in search of high-value species. Photo courtesy of Chamari Dissanayake[23].

In the 1980s, after the introduction of snorkeling and SCUBA diving techniques, divers were able to move into the deep waters. This helped in expansion of fishing activities on the eastern, northeastern, and southern coasts of the country.

Even today, sea cucumber harvesting is done without any special gear or net. Sea cucumbers are hand-picked by the SCUBA or Skin-divers who dive from fiberglass reinforced plastic motorboats. The harvesting takes place during the day as well as nighttime. The boats leave early in the morning and return with the harvest by late afternoon. In the nighttime, the boats leave early in the evening and return at dawn. [24]

Geography

Places where it is grown

There are about 1000 fishing villages along the 1770 km long coast of Sri Lanka. Sea cucumber, which is known as *Muhudu Pipinna* in Sri Lanka, is found along its Northern (Jaffna Lagoon), eastern (Trincomalee, Kalmunaei, Pothuwil) and northwestern (Putlam to Mannar) coasts.

The sea cucumber harvesting is heavily dependent on the seasons. On the Northwestern coast, harvesting takes place from October to April while on the eastern coast, it is harvested intensively during May to September. But this doesn't mean that the sea cucumber farming industry becomes non-operational during the "off-season".

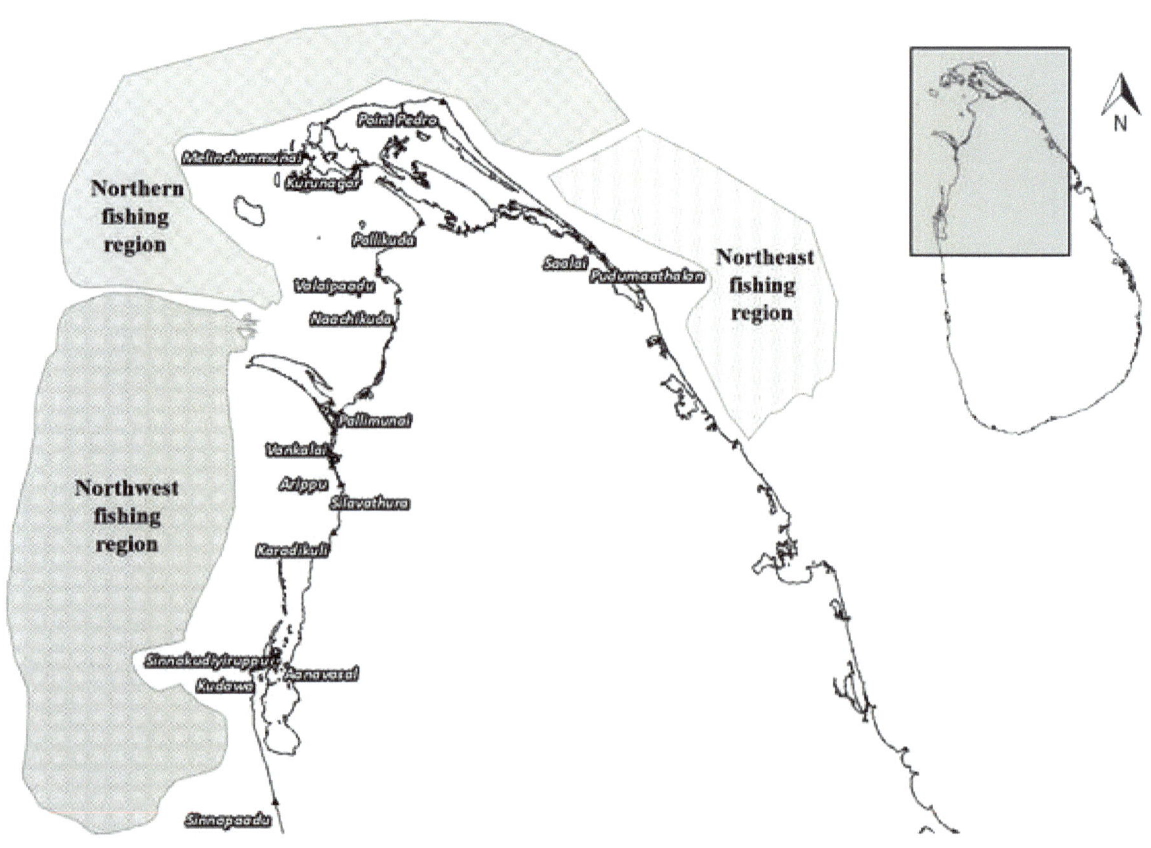

A sea leech hatchery was started in 2016 by a Chinese company centered on the Northern Peninsula, on the coast of Jaffna and Kilinochchi. Other areas that are covered with sea cucumber farming and fencing the sea are Ariyalai – Poompugar, Mandativu, Punguduthivu, Paruthithivu, Mariyamthoddu in Kolumputhurai, Paasaiyur, Kurunagar, Analaitivu, Poonagari, and Kiranchi.

There are two sea cucumber hatcheries in the Northern Province one of which is state-owned and started operations in Mannar a few months ago. In further North, Pungudutivu, where the new farm is being proposed, is in close proximity to Nainativu. This is one of the three islands Sri Lanka cleared for a Chinese renewable energy project last year. This is one of the pretexts China has been using to increase its influence in the Indian ocean.

Traditional fishing ground for SL fishermen

There are three major sectors of fishing in Sri Lanka –

1. **Marine Fisheries** – The marine area from shore to the edge of the continental shelf is referred to as the coastal sub-sector. Fishing in this area are generally concluded under a single day operation. This sector contributes the most to the total fish catch with coastal fish catch being about 60 percent of it.

2. **Inland fisheries** – This type of fishing takes place in rivers, lakes, ponds, marshes, lagoons. Capture fishing in irrigation tanks and reservoirs is an expanding economic activity that provides cheap animal protein, income, and employment for rural people.

3. **Deep-sea fishing** – The area beyond the continental shelf extending up to the Exclusive Economic Zone is referred to as Off-shore and Deep-sea subsector. Fishing in the high seas can take multiple days of operation. Travelers of fishers who would engage in this deep-sea fishing activity will have to spend a few hours at the middle sea.

Major fish species caught in Sri Lankan waters are skipjack, blood fish, yellow fin tuna, mullet, shark, trevally, Spanish mackerel, prawns, lobsters.

Major fishing harbours of Sri Lanka are Ambalangoda, Beruwala, Chilaw, Dodanduwa, Dickowita North, Dickowita South, Galle, Hambantota, Hikkaduwa, Kalpitiya, Kirinda, Kudawella, Mirissa, Negombo, Nilwella, Panadura, Puranawella, Suduwella, Tangalle, Trincomalee and Valachchenai.

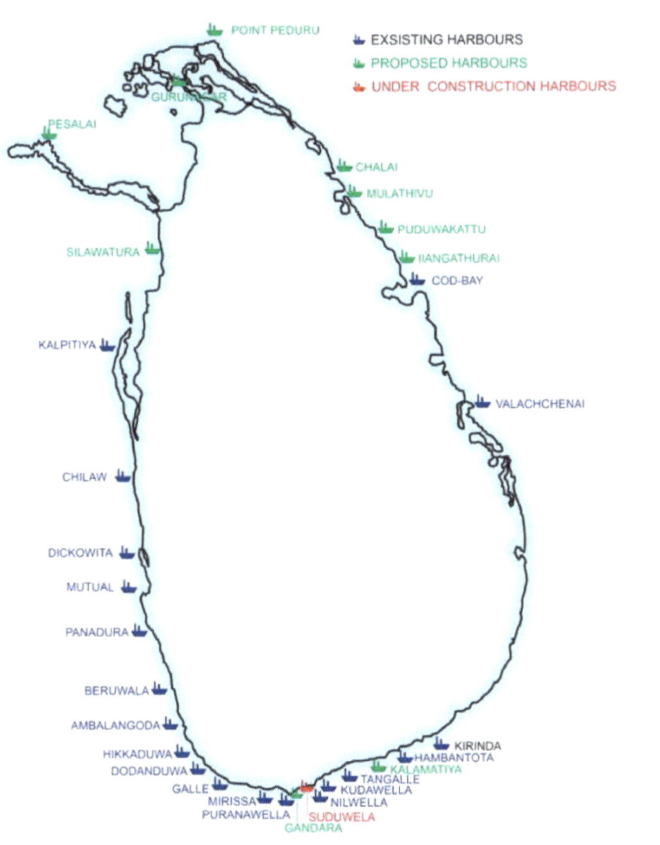

Map: Ceylon Fishery Harbours Corporation(CFHC)[25]

Economy

Cost of sea cucumber in 2010 and 2020.

As per online resources, the approximate price range for Sri Lankan Sea Cucumber is between US$ 30.39 and US$ 54.69 per kilogram or between US$ 13.78 and US$ 24.81 per pound (lb) in 2022. In 2017, a kilo of sea cucumber was priced at US$21.64 and in 2019 the price went up to $30.39 per kilo.[26] According to a January 2020 *Hindustan Times* report, a kilo of sea cucumbers can fetch about Rs. 50,000 and some fishermen could even earn Rs. 2 lakhs in a single day. [27]

While in the 1980s, sea cucumbers were priced at less than £50 a kilo, the prices nowadays have risen to more than £200 a kilo. The rarer species such as *Holothuria scabra, H. nobilis and Holothuria fuscogilva,* which are found primarily in Northern and Northwester regions, can even fetch 2,500 pounds for a kilo.

The Japanese sea cucumber (*Apostichopus japonicus*) is currently the most expensive species on the market at a staggering cost of US$3,500 per kilogram.

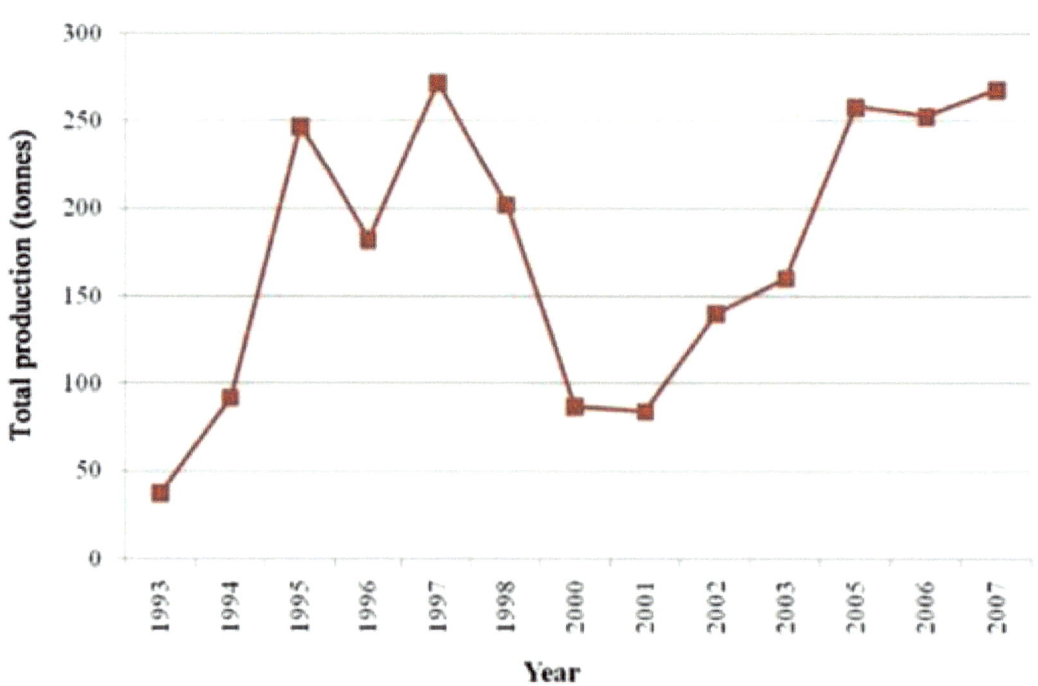

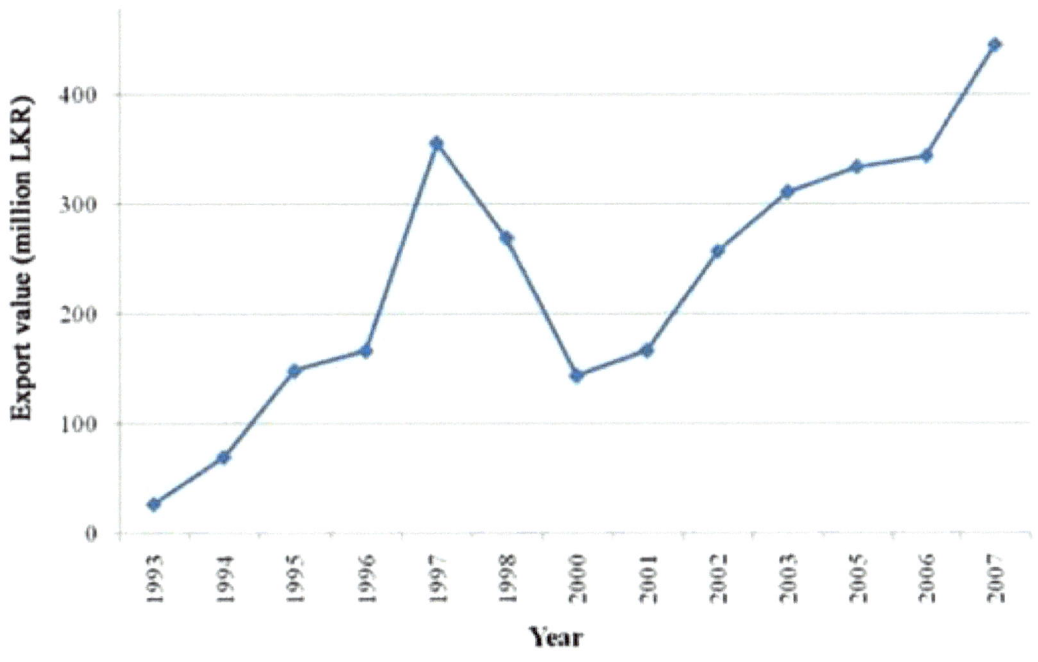

28

How could such large farms pop after 2016?

Before 2015, the Ministry responsible for coastal conservation was interested in sea cucumber farming with the goal of helping the fishing community. Promotions and campaigns weaved around increasing sea cucumber farming were run.

The National Aquatic Resources Research and Development Agency (NARA) began identifying locations for sea cucumber farming in 2015 using scientific methods. Several isolated sea cucumber breeding sites in the North were identified. A Gazette notification was issued on sea cucumber farming in 2015 and around 10,000 acres were identified and proposed.[29]

In June 2022, the Sri Lankan cabinet approved a proposal for a large-scale commercial sea leech and sea cucumber farming project spanning 5,000 acres in the districts of Jaffna, Mannar, Kilinochchi and Batticaloa in the Northern and

Eastern Provinces. The government also plans to set up an export village in an area of 100 acres.

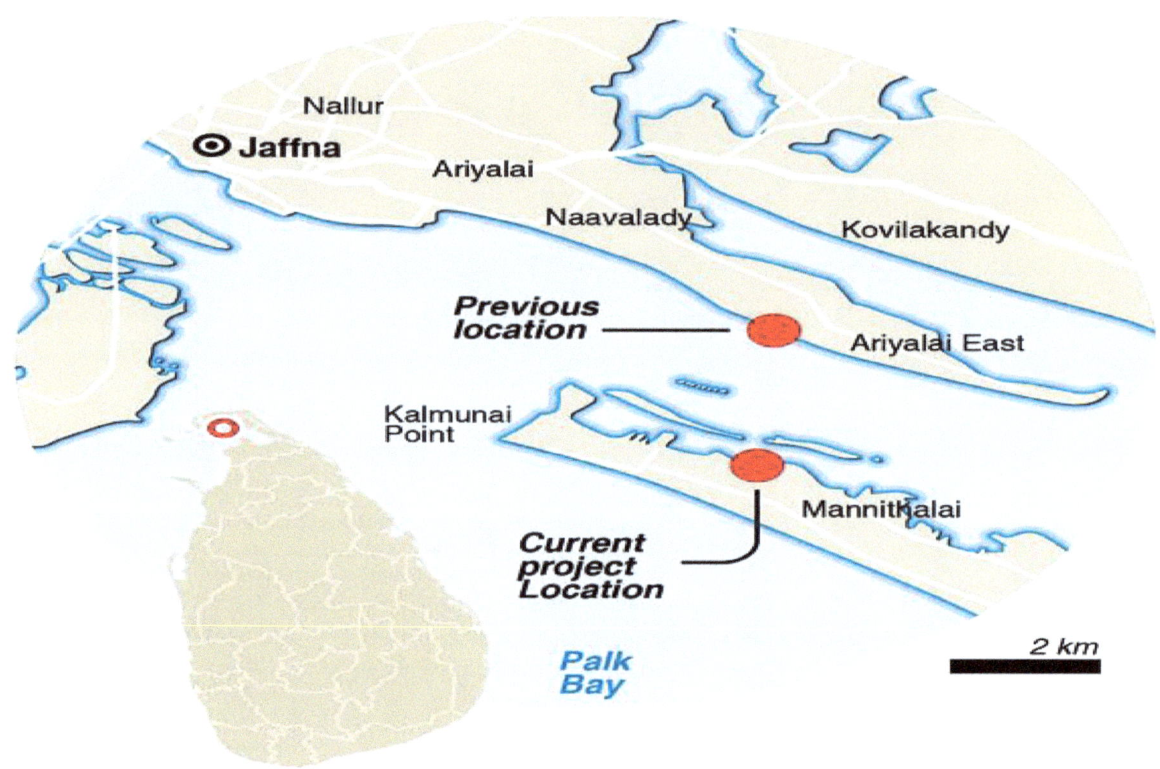

Entry of Chinese fishing company

While India banned sea cucumber farming back in 2001 under the Indian Wildlife Protection Act of 1972, harvesting of sea cucumber is legal in Sri Lanka under a licensing system.

In 2016, a sea leech hatchery was established by a Chinese joint venture company 'Gui Lan (Pvt) Ltd' centered on the northern peninsula to facilitate the export of these species to China. The company was registered as a private limited liability company with a registered address in Negombo with two Chinese and a Sri Lankan being named as directors in April 2016. One of the several partners is Steven Gong who belongs to Taiwan but has been living in Sri Lanka for three decades. Other partners and investors of the hatchery are also from China.

Steven Gong, a Taiwanese partner in the Chinese-owned Gui Lan sea cucumber hatchery, is perplexed by the furore his business has created © Rubatheesan Sandran[30]

Gui Lan (Pvt) Ltd operates a hatchery and a nursery where baby animals are nursed for up to four months before they are sold to commercial farms run by locals. In addition, the company has opened another nursery in Kowtharimunai, a coastal village in Pooneryn divisional secretariat in Northern Sri Lanka, as a part of its expansion plan. As the locals do not consume this animal, it is exported to China and other countries once the sea cucumber has matured enough.

Why China loves sea cucumbers and leeches?

Considered a delicacy in China since the Ming dynasty, sea cucumbers are often served during banquets and dinners. For Chinese people, it is a symbol of luxury and affluence, which is often showcased on special occasions like weddings and New Year celebrations. It is consumed in many forms, ranging from raw to pickled, spiced, fried, and mixed with other seafood and stews. Dried sea cucumber, also known as *bêche-de-mer* or trepan, is used in recipes like soups, stews, and stir-fries.

In Chinese traditional medicine (TCM), sea cucumbers are believed to have medicinal properties which promote and even restore good health. Chinese people use sea cucumbers as a treatment for joint problems like arthritis, to cure impotence, enhance sports performance as it is known to have anti-fatigue effects. In addition, various claims have been made by TCM practitioners about sea cucumber and its extracts about it having unique abilities to treat specific cancers, reduce blood clots, and increase the longevity of consumers.

All these factors have made sea cucumbers one of the most expensive seafood items that already have a vast market available for business. According to reports, between 1996 and 2011, the number of countries exporting sea cucumbers increased from 35 to 83.[31] The demand for sea cucumbers has been on the rise, which has led to the construction of massive farms along the Lankan coastline.

Cost of SC and SU per KG in China

While the number of countries engaged in sea cucumber harvesting has increased, the overall number of sea cucumbers has decreased worldwide. This has led to the species becoming even more expensive over the years.

According to Selina Wamucii, an online food and agricultural product aggregator, before 2019, one kilo of sea cucumbers was going for US$169.12 in 2017 and US$399.66 in 2018. In 2019 the export price changed to $983.33 per kilo, increasing by 146.045 per cent.

In 2022, the approximate price range for China Sea Cucumbers was between US$ 983.47 and US$ 399.66 per kilogram or between US$ 446.1 and US$ 181.28 per pound (lb.).

The price in Yuan Renminbi is CNY 6389.05 per kg. The average price for a ton is US$ 983466.67 in Shanghai and Beijing.

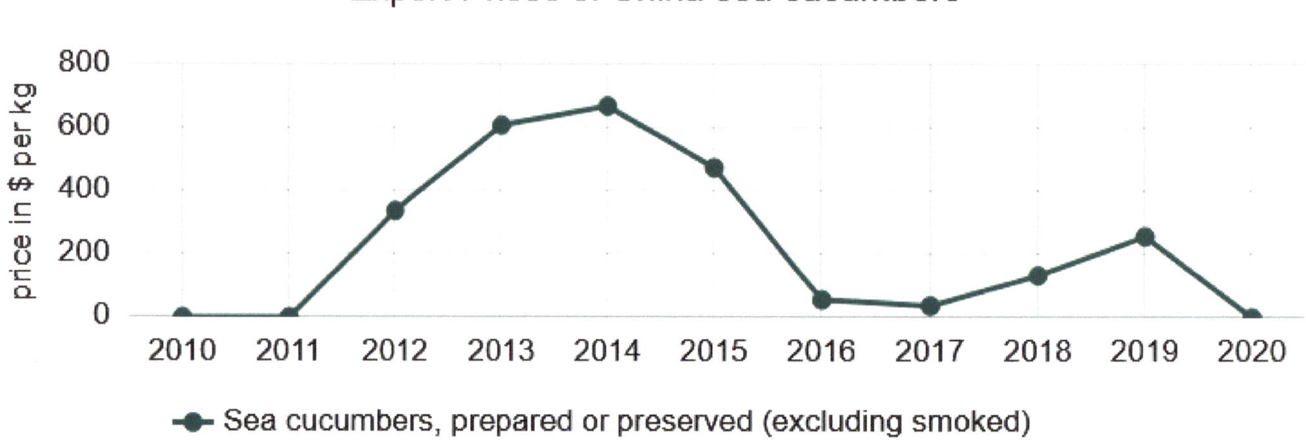

China's import price for sea cucumbers in 2019 was US$36.18 per kilogram.[32]

However, the market prices of sea urchins have been reduced. Before 2019, a kg of sea urchins was going for US$62.33 in 2017 and US$59.26 in 2018. In 2019 the export price changed to $52.20 per kilo, by -11.921%. China's import price for sea urchins in 2019 was US$21.39 per kilogram.[33]

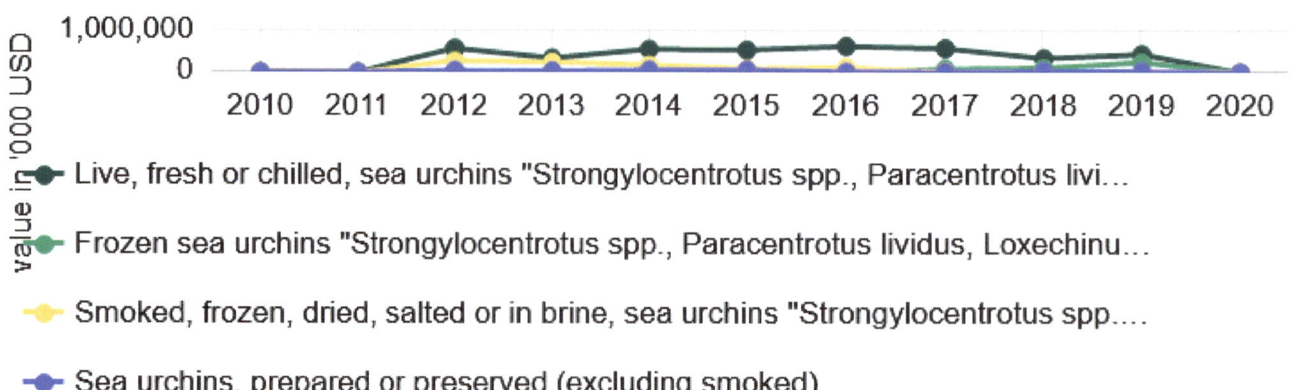

Export Prices of China sea urchins

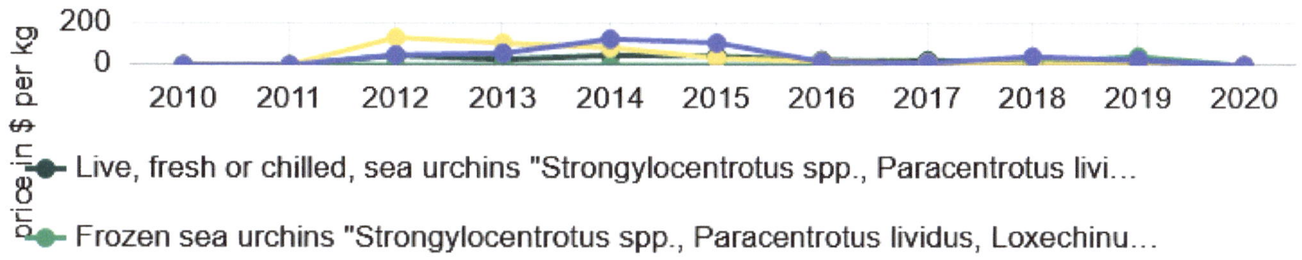

● Live, fresh or chilled, sea urchins "Strongylocentrotus spp., Paracentrotus livi…

● Frozen sea urchins "Strongylocentrotus spp., Paracentrotus lividus, Loxechinu…

● Smoked, frozen, dried, salted or in brine, sea urchins "Strongylocentrotus spp.…

● Sea urchins, prepared or preserved (excluding smoked)

Issues

According to an article published by *Daily Mirror*, in 2020 alone, Sri Lanka exported about 326 tons of sea urchins, with China being the biggest buyer.[34] Such a mass-scale operation has led to many socio-economic and environmental issues in the country.

1. **Illegal marine areas capturing** - The fishermen of the Northern Province in Sri Lanka have been protesting on the establishment of illegal sea cucumber farms. Over 5,000 acres have been allocated for sea cucumber framing. However, according to the TU findings, over 200 sea cucumber farms that are in operation are unlicensed. There are 90 sea cucumber farms in the Jaffna DS alone, and only 48 have permits. The establishment of Gui Lan (Pvt) Ltd.'s new nursery has led to acres of sea-land being fenced off for sea cucumber harvesting, shutting out the traditional fishermen who harvest prawns for a living.

    1.1. **Electrified fence** – Chinese companies like Gui Lan have constructed several sea cucumber farms with electric fences along the seashore, restricting the movement of other aquatic species towards the coast, especially during monsoon season. The large nets on the shallow waters of the sea for sea cucumber farming prevent the breeding of fish, crabs, and prawns. In Kayts Grama Seva Division, 3,480 acres of sea and land have been fenced for sea cucumber farming. This malevolent practice could pose a severe threat to the long-term sustainability of the region.

    1.2. **Illegal establishment** – It has come to light that the Gui Lan joint venture has failed to secure a permit from the National Aquaculture Development Authority of Sri Lanka (NAQDA) for its new nursery in Kowtharimunai in Pooneryin. This new nursery is located a few kilometres from its Ariyalai hatchery in Jaffna. Similarly, only two farms were approved in Kiranchi, whereas there are 40 sea cucumber farms in that area, it has been highlighted. This makes most of the sea cucumber farms illegal in the North.[35]

    1.3. **Illegal expansion of area** – At present, there are four ways through which juvenile sea cucumbers are reared – indoor facilities, pond cultures, sea ranching and pen cultures. Except for indoor facilities, all other methods depend on tide and hydrodynamics. In order to take the most benefit of these natural phenomena, the boundary lines of the sea cucumber farms keep changing.

1.4. Local fishermen bodies were not informed – The Vinayagar Fishermen Co-operative Society, a local fishermen group in Pooneryn, rejected reports that it had granted its consent for the construction of the Kowtharimunai sea cucumber nursery. Jaffna District Fisheries Union Federation President Annalingam Annarasa told *Ceylon Today* that NARA, since 1972, has never conducted research in the Northern Sea. He also pointed out that it was only a GPS waypoint offered to NAQDA, but a sea cucumber farming system wasn't studied. He said NARA did not inform anything about such plans for sea cucumber farming. It was only on 25 November 2022 that two social and economic enhancement teams came to conduct a social impact assessment.

2. **Issues faced by local fishermen** – Extreme poverty and low incomes during the fishing season have pushed artisanal fishers to harvest sea cucumbers despite the ban. Unlike in the past, artisanal fishers are forced to sell their harvest at lower prices to traders, while state authorities label them criminals. Artisanal fishers in the region have held several protests and taken legal action demanding the government lift the ban on sea cucumber harvesting but in vain. They also demand that the state control and regulate trawling, which impacts sea cucumber populations more than their traditional livelihoods.

2.1. Destruction of livelihood and a number of families affected – In Sri Lanka, about 3,200 small-scale fishing families have been seriously affected by the creation of sea leech farms, losing their livelihoods during an ongoing economic crisis in the country. The fishermen point out that out of 100 fishermen if 10 establish a sea leech farm, the livelihood of the remaining 90 who catch shrimp, prawns and other fishes is at stake.

2.2. Lack of access to the traditional fishing ground – A group of fishermen also started a hunger strike near the Kiranchi fishing harbour because the road leading to their boats for fishing activities has been blocked due to the permission of a group of fishermen to set up sea leech cultivation boxes. In addition, the fencing off acres of sea land for sea cucumber harvesting is shutting traditional fishermen, especially the ones engaged in prawn harvesting, from pursuing a livelihood.

2.3. Only a few local fishermen are employed as daily wage earners. Out of the 17,000 fishing families living in the Northern Province, less than 1000 have been selected to work in these farms, leaving the remaining 16,000 Dhiwara(fishing) families at risk of losing their livelihood. This has led to continuous protests demanding the closure of the illegal sea leech farms in the Punagari, Kirawan and Ilavankuda areas.

3. <u>**Destruction of marine diversity**</u> – Sea cucumbers help detoxify contaminants in the soil and other environments and help in nutrient cycling and redistribution of sediments. Moreover, they help other species, such as corals, to live, making them ideal for bioremediation. But the effect of these farms on marine diversity and ecology has been grave. The water has become murkier and more polluted in coastal areas where the sea cucumber population has declined due to over-fishing.

3.1. Large-scale farming using artificial means/hatchery – In order to run a sea cucumber farm, wild sea cucumbers are caught from the sea and placed in the farms and hatcheries. This creates an ecological imbalance in the ocean. At the hatchery, high levels of electricity, fuel and water are required during the feeding stage to maintain the culturing water temperature and oxygen status for juvenile sea cucumbers, which has a significant environmental impact. In addition, high levels of fossil fuel emissions from energy use, large amounts of nitrogen and phosphorus discharged in wastewater, and a low utilisation rate of post-production waste contribute to pollution in the farm area.

3.2. The lower number of prawns, crabs, and squid – Traditional fishermen are fighting for survival as the shallow waters of the sea are netted with huge nets, allowing juvenile sea cucumbers to grow. Hence the breeding of fish, prawns, and crabs is fast disappearing. In addition, the lights aimed at the sea urchin production farms across the lagoon are switched on in the evening, affecting fish and prawns' movement towards the shore. These organisms live near the coast or move towards the sea, depending on the salinity of the waters. Cultivation of sea leeches in this way without proper planning and proper study has raised many obvious problems, especially in the sea areas where shrimps, crabs and squids breed naturally.

Conclusion

The Sri Lankan government would need to immediately address the illegal and unregulated sea cucumber farming, which has severely impacted the island's marine ecology. The traditional fisheries industry has been directly affected. There is a need for immediate implementation of a holistic sea cucumber management plan to ensure the sustainability of this resource in future or a complete ban on sea cucumber and sea leech farmers operating without a license from the relevant government authorities. The political influence to operate unregulated Chinese sea cucumber farming, which impedes government regulators from carrying out their duty, requires considerable attention from the public and media to expose and strengthen the regulatory mechanisms to protect the marine environment. China's back channel economic interest in the northern waters will further complicate the relationship with India and Indian national security if the domestic foreign policy ignores the growing Chinese influence in Sri Lanka. Sri Lanka already faces a considerable threat from Chinese land acquisitions from long-term lease agreements in Hambanthota port and Colombo Port City, where none of these agreements was made available to the public. While environmental impact assessments for most Chinese projects have raised concerns, such as Mattala airport being built near a wildlife sanctuary, the challenges to the marine environment would require immediate attention. Host governments should assess the geoeconomic interest of China with the long-term geopolitical objectives China wish to achieve in the geo and marine sphere in smaller littorals in the Indian ocean.

References

[1] Ceylon Fishery Harbours Corporation (CFHC), http://www.cfhc.gov.lk

[2] The National Aquatic Resources Research and Development Agency (NARA), http://www.nara.ac.lk

[3] https://oceansasia.org/why-sea-cucumbers/

[4] https://www.un.org/depts/los/clcs_new/submissions_files/submission_lka_43_2009.htm

[5] UN, *Submission by the Democratic Socialist Republic of Sri Lanka*,
https://www.ft.lk/Business/blue-ocean-economy-the-future-prosperity-of-sri-lanka-lies-in-the-sea/34-234338

[6] Maritime Boundaries Geodatabase, *Flanders Marine Institute*,
https://www.researchgate.net/figure/Map-of-the-Sri-Lankan-Exclusive-Economic-Zone-EEZ-Source-Maritime-Boundaries_fig1_313525677

[7] *Author's interview with Ambassador Mahinda Samarasinghe at the Sri Lankan embassy in Washington DC*, 21 Sep 2022. Ambassador Samarasinghe was the Minister of ports and shipping during the agreement signing of Hambanthota in 2017.

[8] Shepard, Wade. *The Story Behind the World's Emptiest International Airport*, 2016. *Forbes*. 05 28. Accessed 2023, https://www.forbes.com/sites/wadeshepard/2016/05/28/the-story-behind-the-worlds-emptiest-international-airport-sri-lankas-mattala-rajapaksa/?sh=699a58b37cea

[9] Sonia Sarkar, SCMP, *As Indian trawlers steal Sri Lankan fish, Chinese sea cucumber firm offers a lifeline*, 4th Sep 2022,
https://www.scmp.com/week-asia/economics/article/3191231/indian-trawlers-steal-sri-lankan-fish-chinese-sea-cucumber-firm

[10] Environmental Justice Foundation, *The Ever-Widening Net: Mapping the Scale, Nature and Corporate Structures of Illegal, Unreported and Unregulated Fishing by the Chinese Distant-Water Fleet*, London, United Kingdom, March 2022, p. 11.

[11] Derek Grossman, RAND, *China's gambit in the Pacific, Testimony presented before the U.S.-China Economic and Security Review Commission on August 3, 2022*,
https://www.rand.org/content/dam/rand/pubs/testimonies/CTA2100/CTA2198-1/RAND_CTA2198-1.pdf

[12] Adam Somers, "Chinese Fishing Boat Stripped and Escorted Out of Palau," *Island Times*, January 5, 2021.

[13] Dan Southerland, "Chinese Overfishing in the South Pacific Devastates Some Islands' Livelihoods," Radio Free Asia, April 6, 2021.

[14] Jaime Moreno, "China's Fishing Fleet Threatens the Galapagos Islands," Voice of America, November 3, 2021.

[15] Malaka Rodrigo, Pragati Prava, *Demand for sea cucumbers turns India-Sri Lanka waters into trafficking hotspot*, 11th Feb 2022, https://india.mongabay.com/2022/02/demand-for-sea-cucumbers-turns-india-sri-lanka-waters-into-trafficking-hotspot/

[16] Daily FT, *Chinese Ambassador Qi Zhenhong wraps up successful visit to Northern Province,* January1st2022, https://www.ft.lk/news/Chinese-Ambassador-Qi-Zhenhong-wraps-up-successful-visit-to-Northern-Province/56-728486

[17] WHOI, *Sea Urchins*, https://www.whoi.edu/science/B/people/kamaral/SeaUrchins.html

[18] Lance E. Morgan, Scoresby A. Shepherd, *Population and Spatial Structure of Two Common Temperate Reef Herbivores: Abalone and Sea Urchins,* Editor(s): Jacob P. Kritzer, Peter F. Sale,Marine Metapopulations, Academic Press, 2006, Pages 205-246, https://doi.org/10.1016/B978-012088781-1/50009-1.

[19] NAQDA, 'The first commercial sea cucumber hatchery, http://www.naqda.gov.lk/news/The-first-commercial-sea-cucumber-hatchery#gallery-4

[20] Malaka Rodrigo, Pragati Prava, *Demand for sea cucumbers turns India-Sri Lanka waters into trafficking hotspot*, 11th Feb 2022, https://india.mongabay.com/2022/02/demand-for-sea-cucumbers-turns-india-sri-lanka-waters-into-trafficking-hotspot/

[21] Sandranathan Rubatheesan , *Sea Cucumber Farming Spells Death to Traditional Coastal Fishing in Northern Sri Lanka*, Earth Journalism Network, 09 March 2022, https://earthjournalism.net/stories/sea-cucumber-farming-spells-death-to-traditional-coastal-fishing-in-northern-sri-lanka

[22] The Hindu, Freediving in the Palk Bay, https://frontline.thehindu.com/social-issues/general-issues/article10073992.ece/photo/7/

[23] Malaka Rodrigo, Pragati Prava, *Demand for sea cucumbers turns India-Sri Lanka waters into trafficking hotspot*, 11th Feb 2022, https://india.mongabay.com/2022/02/demand-for-sea-cucumbers-turns-india-sri-lanka-waters-into-trafficking-hotspot/

[24] D.C.T. Dissanayake, Sujeewa Athukoorala, '*Present status of the sea cucumber fishery in Sri Lanka'*,January 2010, Research Gate, https://www.researchgate.net/publication/238745388_Present_status_of_the_sea_cucumber_fishery_in_Sri_Lanka

[25] Ceylon Fishery Harbours Corporation (CFHC), http://www.cfhc.gov.lk/Harbour_Main.php

[26] Selina Vamucii, Export market prices for Sri Lanka Sea cucumber, https://www.selinawamucii.com/insights/prices/sri-lanka/sea-cucumber/

[27] Chatterjee, Badri,"219 sea cucumbers worth Rs1.17 crore seized in largest seizure in Lakshadweep", Hindustan Times, 15.01.2020 https://www.hindustantimes.com/mumbai-news/219-sea-cucumbers-worth-rs1-17-crore-seized-in-largest-seizure-in-lakshadweep/story-O20FnMsd3bSd4HE6HMbYPK.html

[28] D.C.T. Dissanayake, Sujeewa Athukoorala, '*Present status of the sea cucumber fishery in Sri Lanka*' ,January 2010, Research Gate, https://www.researchgate.net/publication/238745388_Present_status_of_the_sea_cucumber_fishery_in_Sri_Lanka

[29] Sulochana Ramiah Mohan, Mushrooming sea cucumber farms hinder Northern fishers, 24th Dec 2022,https://ceylontoday.lk/2022/12/24/mushrooming-sea-cucumber-farms-hinder-northern-fishers/

[30] Benjamin Parkin, *Sea cucumbers feed China's influence in Sri Lanka*, 22nd Feb 2022, https://www.ft.com/content/d67e1f47-754e-4c0f-a35f-f28c706cf0bc

[31] Nathaniel Lee and Shira Polan, *Sea cucumbers are so valuable that people are risking their lives diving for them*, 1st Oct 2020, https://www.businessinsider.com/why-sea-cucumbers-so-expensive-seafood-2019-1?r=US&IR=T

[32] Selina Vamucii, Export market prices for Sri Lanka Sea cucumber, https://www.selinawamucii.com/insights/prices/sri-lanka/sea-cucumber/

[33] Selina Wamucii, *China sea urchin's prices*, https://www.selinawamucii.com/insights/prices/china/sea-urchins/

[34] Majueran, Maya, "Chinese Investment in Sea Cucumber Farm in Sri Lanka also a Threat to Indian Security?",Daily Mirror, 20.10.2022 https://www.dailymirror.lk/news-features/Chinese-Investment-in-Sea-Cucumber-Farm-in-Sri-Lanka-also-a-Threat-to-Indian-Security/131-247136

[35] Sulochana Ramiah Mohan, Mushrooming sea cucumber farms hinder Northern fishers, 24th Dec 2022,https://ceylontoday.lk/2022/12/24/mushrooming-sea-cucumber-farms-hinder-northern-fishers/

Author Bio: *Asanga Abeyagoonasekera is an international security and geopolitics analyst and strategic advisor from Sri Lanka. He is the Executive Director of the South Asia Foresight Network (SAFN) under Millennium Project. He serves as a Senior Fellow to the Millennium Project in Washington DC. He was the former Chairman of the Government Fishery Harbours Corporation from 2005-2010 and served as the Director at Sri Lanka Ports Authority. During his tenure at fisheries, he worked with coastal engineers, marine scientists, and researchers. With almost two decades of experience in the government sector in advisory positions to working at foreign policy and defence think tanks, he was the Founding Director General of the National Security Think Tank under the Ministry of Defence (INSSSL) until January 2020. Earlier, he served as Executive Director at Kadirgamar Institute (LKIIRSS). He is the author of Teardrop Diplomacy (2023) published by Bloomsbury in 2023 Conundrum of an Island (2021), Sri Lanka at Crossroads (2019) and Towards a Better World Order (2015). He was recognized as a Young Global Leader by the World Economic Forum.*

South Asia Foresight Network (SAFN)

South Asia Foresight Network (SAFN) functions under The Millennium Project in Washington DC, with representatives from Afghanistan, Bangladesh, Bhutan, India, Maldives, Nepal, Pakistan, and Sri Lanka. SAFN's purpose is to create a regional foresight capacity for joint futures research to improve cooperation and synergies among all nations of the region.

SAFN
SOUTH ASIA FORESIGHT NETWORK